FUN·TO·MAKE CRAFTS FOR CHRISTMAS

Boyds Mills Press

Editor

Tom Daning

Craft Contributors

Robin Adams
Sharon Addy
Martha Utley Aitken
Beverly Blasucci
Linda Bloomgren
Debra Boyles
Doris D. Breiholz
Dorothy Anderson Burge
Marie Cecchini
Tanya Easterling Clark
Lydia Cutler
Ronni Davis
Cory A. Derr
Ruth Dougherty
Donna Dowdy
Kathryn H. Dulan
Kathy Everett

Susan M. Fisher
Kelly McCumber Freihofer
Dorothy L. Getchell
Edna Harrington
Marguerite Harrington
Mark Haverstock
Isabel K. Hobba
Carmen Horn
Rebecca Hubka
Verlie Hutchens
Joan Hyman
Ellen Javernick
Helen Jeffries
Murley K. Kight
Roseanne Kirby
Jean Kuhn
Jean LaWall

Lee Lindeman
Dorothy Scott Milke
Nancy Mobley
Shari O'Rourke
Kathy Paul
James W. Perrin Jr.
Glenda Powers
Jane K. Priewe
Kathy Ross
Laura Sassi
Becky Sawyer
Lois Saxelby
Dorothy Snethen
Carle Statter
Linda M. Thurlow
Sherry Timberman
Sharon Dunn Umnik

Agnes Choate Wonson
D. A. Woodliff
Rebecca D. Zurawski

Craft Builder

Verlie Hutchens

Copyright © 2005 by Boyds Mills Press
All rights reserved

Published by Boyds Mills Press, Inc.
A Highlights Company
815 Church Street
Honesdale, Pennsylvania 18431
Printed in China

Publisher Cataloging-in-Publication Data

Fun-to-make crafts for Christmas / Boyds Mills Press.—1st ed.
[64] p.: col. photos. ; cm.
Includes index.
Summary: Includes step-by-step directions to make decorations, gifts, and
    greeting cards for Christmas.
ISBN 1-59078-342-5
ISBN 1-59078-367-0 (pbk.)
1. Christmas decorations. 2. Handicraft. I. Title.
745.594/12 22   TT900.C4.B54 2005

First edition, 2005
Book designed by Janet Moir McCaffrey
The text of this book is set in 11-point New Century Schoolbook.

Visit our Web site at www.boydsmillspress.com

10 9 8 7 6 5 4 3 2 1 hc
10 9 8 7 6 5 4 3 2 1 pb

In these pages you will find 150 imaginative craft ideas for Christmas and winter. Gifts, games, toys, decorations, greeting cards—whatever you want to make, it's here. So put on your most stylish paint-splattered smock, roll up your sleeves, and create. Soon, St. Nick will be coming down your chimney!

Safety First

Although most crafts in this book are designed for you to make yourself, remember to ask for an adult's help when handling sharp instruments or using the stove.

Follow the Directions—But Add Your Own Flair

To build each craft, follow the steps listed. The directions and the pictures are helpful guides, but they are no substitute for your own imagination. You might figure out a different way to make an angel or to decorate your Christmas wreath. Or you might be inspired to make up your own crafts.

Neatness Counts

Before you get crafty, be smart and cover your work area. Old newspapers, brown paper bags, old sheets, or a plastic drop cloth will work. Protect your clothes with an apron, a smock, or a big old shirt. And remember to clean up after you are finished.

Stock Your Craft Workshop

We've included a list of materials to make each craft. Recyclable items such as cardboard tubes, old socks, and paper bags are needed for many of them. Before you start, check out the items in the materials list for the crafts you plan to make. Ask your parents, friends, and relatives to start saving these things for you, so you will always have a supply on hand. If you don't have the exact item listed, something else may work just as well. Make sure you clean and dry the recyclables before using them. Also, good crafters usually keep some supplies handy—such as scissors, crayons, markers, craft glue, tape, pens, pencils, paint, a hole punch, and a stapler. Because these are used so frequently, we don't include them in the list of materials.

Have Fun!

Felt Ornament

felt ● fabric paint ● ribbon ● sequins ● glitter ● spring-type clothespin

1. Cut out a simple holiday shape from felt.
2. Decorate one side with fabric paint, or glue on ribbon, sequins, or glitter. Let dry.
3. Glue the back to the flat side of a spring-type clothespin. When dry, color the rest of the clothespin.
4. Clip the ornament to a tree branch.

Butter-Box Sleigh

butter box ● felt ● rickrack ● cardboard

1. Cut off the top of a butter box. Cut a curved section out of each long side. Trim a bit off one end.
2. Cover the sleigh with felt and add rickrack.
3. Cut two runners from cardboard and paint them black.
4. Curl the front ends up, and glue them to your sleigh.

Pinecone Christmas Tree

plastic-foam cone ● felt ● small and large pinecones ● ball ornaments

1. Cover a plastic-foam cone with felt and let dry.
2. Starting at the bottom of the cone, glue on small pinecones. Continue around the cone, adding shiny ball ornaments. You may want to let a small section dry before you continue.
3. When you reach the top of the cone, add a larger pinecone with glue.

Stenciled Sweatshirt

cardboard ● red sweatshirt ● green fabric paint ● needle ● embroidery floss ● buttons

1. Draw and cut out a tree shape from the center of a piece of cardboard, making a stencil.
2. Lay a red sweatshirt flat on your work surface. Place another piece of cardboard inside the sweatshirt. Tape the stencil on the front of the sweatshirt. Paint the inside of the stencil with green fabric paint. Follow the directions on the paint bottle for drying time.
3. With a needle and embroidery floss, sew different-colored buttons of different sizes all over the tree as ornaments.

Snowman Centerpiece

white paper bag ● newspaper ● paper ● glitter

1. Stuff a white paper bag with crumpled newspaper. Fold down the top and tape it closed.
2. For the brim of the hat, cut out a large black paper circle and glue it on top of the bag. Cut out two wide strips of black paper. Turn under the ends of each one and glue them onto the brim as shown.
3. Cut out a paper hatband, place it around the hat, and tape the ends together. Add a paper holly leaf and berries.
4. Create eyes and a scarf from paper. Use a hole punch to make circles for the mouth. For the nose, roll an orange paper triangle to form a cone, tape it, and trim the ends. Glue everything onto the bag.
5. Place your snowman on newspaper. For "snow," add dots of glue to the snowman, then sprinkle glitter on them. Let dry.

Angel Napkin Ring

paint stirrer ● sandpaper ● chenille sticks ● fabric scraps
● yarn ● wiggle eyes ● felt ● white napkin

1. Ask an adult to cut a paint stirrer in half. Use sandpaper to smooth rough edges.
2. For the napkin ring, wrap a chenille stick around itself several times. Then tape it to the back of the paint stirrer.
3. Cut a fabric rectangle. Stretch and glue it around the stick to look like an angel's robe. Add yarn hair, wiggle eyes, and details with felt and marker. Twist a yellow chenille stick into a halo and glue it to the back. Let dry.
4. Fold a white paper napkin to make pleats. Slide it through the napkin ring to look like angel wings.

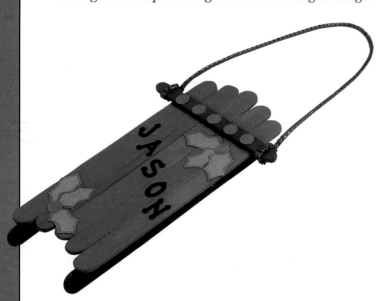

Sled Ornament

craft sticks ● sticker letters ● paper ● cording

1. Glue five craft sticks together for the sled frame. Glue a smaller craft stick on the frame for the handles.
2. Glue two craft sticks to the bottom of the sled for runners.
3. Paint the sled and let dry. Add your name with sticker letters. Glue on paper decorations and cording for a hanger.

Reindeer Finger Puppet

old brown cotton glove ● paper ● ribbon

1. To make the puppet, cut off a finger from an old brown cotton glove. With a hole punch, punch out two white paper dots for eyes and a red paper dot for the nose. Glue these to one side of the fingertip to form the facial features.
2. From light brown paper, cut out antlers and glue them to the back of the fingertip. Make a bow tie from ribbon and paper, and glue in place.
3. Place your finger in the glove finger to work your reindeer puppet.

St. Nick
Door Decoration

corrugated cardboard ● fabric ● white plastic table cover
● paper ● 1½-inch plastic-foam ball ● string

1. For St. Nick's body, cut a large triangle from corrugated cardboard. Starting at the point of the triangle, staple or tape red fabric for the hat, beige fabric for the head, and red fabric for the body.
2. For the hat brim, cut a cardboard strip and cover it with a section cut from a white plastic table cover. Staple it to the hat.
3. Cut a cardboard beard shape and cover it with white plastic. Cut strips of plastic, loop them, and staple them to the beard.
4. Add paper eyes and eyebrows. For the nose, paint a 1½-inch plastic-foam ball red and glue it in place. Cut boots from cardboard and cover with black fabric.
5. Glue a loop of string to the back. Hang your St. Nick where he won't get wet.

Greeting-Card Nativity

cardboard tube ● old holiday greeting cards ● heavy cardboard ● dried grass, hay, or straw

1. Using a ruler, mark off 1-inch sections along a cardboard tube. Cut the sections, making 1-inch rings.
2. Cut out figures from old holiday greeting cards. Glue them to the 1-inch tube rings so the figures stand up.
3. Cover a heavy piece of cardboard with glue and dried grass, hay, or straw. Glue the figures in place to form the Nativity scene.

Hot-Potato Snowman

old white crew sock ● cotton ● Christmas "music button"
● string ● felt ● embroidery floss ● pompoms

1. Stuff an old white crew sock with cotton. Tuck a Christmas "music button" into the center of the cotton.
2. Wrap and tie string around the opening. This will make a knob of fabric at the snowman's head.
3. Make a scarf by cutting a 10-inch-by-1½-inch length of red felt. Snip the ends to make fringe. Tie the scarf tightly around the sock to make a snowman's head and body.
4. Cut a 6-inch circle of black felt. Lay the felt over the knob of fabric on the head to create a hat. Use black embroidery floss to sew the hat to the head.
5. Glue on a red pompom for a nose and green pompoms for buttons. Cut and glue on two small felt circles for eyes.
6. Use black floss to stitch on a smile. Stitch on arms using brown floss.
7. To play, sit in a circle with some friends. Have someone press the music button in the snowman's belly to start the music. Pass the snowman from person to person until the music stops.

Christmas Card Magnet

old holiday greeting card ● photograph
● magnetic strip

1. Select an old holiday greeting card with a picture that you like. Cut out the picture from the front of the card.
2. To make a frame (as shown at the top), cut out a door-shaped section on your picture and fold it back, or cut out a window-shaped section. Tape a photograph behind the opening.
3. Glue a piece of magnetic strip on the back.

Paper Christmas Tree

poster board ● construction paper
● star stickers

1. To make the tree trunk, cut a strip of brown poster board to measure 4 inches by 27 inches. Fold 2 inches in from each narrow end. Overlap the folded pieces and tape together, forming a triangular shape that will stand.
2. To make tree branches, cut pieces of green construction paper and glue them to the trunk. Place star stickers on the tree. Add a paper star to the top.

Candle and Pinecones

small wooden candleholder
● old CD ● pinecones
● glitter ● candle

1. Glue a small wooden candleholder to the center of an old CD. Glue pinecones around the candleholder.
2. Brush glue over the pinecones and add glitter.
3. Place a candle in the holder.

Woody the Spoon Elf

paper ● wooden spoon ● felt ● needle and thread
● jingle bell ● foam paper ● cording

1. Glue paper eyes and a mouth to the inside of a wooden spoon. Glue paper ears to the sides.
2. Add small strips of felt for hair. Cut a felt hat and glue in place. Sew a jingle bell to the top of the hat.
3. Cut clothes from felt and glue to the handle of the spoon. Trim with foam paper at the neck and cording at the waist. Add paper hands.

Cookie Cutter Wrapping Paper

paper towels ● water ● aluminum foil pan ● cookie cutter
● paper bag, brown kraft paper, or white paper

1. Stack two paper towels together. Fold these to make a rectangular pad. Dampen the paper towel pad with water and place it into an aluminum foil pan. Spread a layer of paint over the paper towel to complete your paint pad.
2. Press a cookie cutter onto the paint pad, then stamp designs onto a paper bag, brown kraft paper, or white paper. Let dry.
3. Use the paper to wrap special gifts for friends and family members.

Christmas Kite

drinking straws ● paper ● plastic gift bag
● clear packing tape ● ribbon ● string
● empty ribbon spool

1. Using the length of two large-sized drinking straws to measure the sides, draw a square on a piece of paper. Make side triangles by measuring 3½ inches down from the top right corner of the square and then out 5 inches. Mark that point and then draw lines to it from the top and bottom corners of the square. Repeat for the left side.
2. Cut out the paper pattern. Trace it onto a plastic gift bag and cut it out.
3. With clear packing tape, tape the drinking straws along the base of each triangle.
4. For the tail, tape ribbon at the bottom edge of the kite behind each of the straws.
5. Tape one piece of thin ribbon to the left and right triangle points. Tie a string to the center of the ribbon and wrap the end of the string around an empty ribbon spool to make the line.

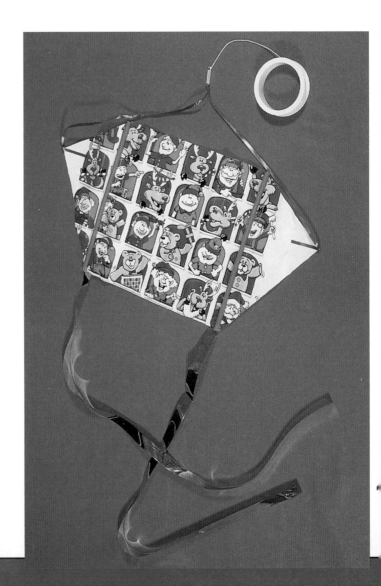

Snowball-Toss Game

rectangular cardboard box ● construction paper
● three 2-inch plastic-foam balls

1. Cover a rectangular cardboard box with construction paper.
2. On a piece of paper, draw a Santa face with a large mouth. Paint or color the face with markers. Glue it to the box and cut out the large mouth.
3. To play, place Santa against the wall. Give each player three tries at throwing 2-inch plastic-foam balls into Santa's mouth. See who can get all three into Santa.

Doily Greetings

construction paper ● paper doilies ● star stickers

1. Cut and fold a piece of construction paper to fit a 4-by-9½-inch envelope.
2. Create trees by cutting cone shapes from paper doilies. Arrange them in a row on the card and glue in place. Add star stickers.
3. Write a Christmas greeting inside.

Doorstop Mouse House

stones ● large cereal box ● construction paper ● string

1. Place some stones inside a large cereal box for weight. Tape the top flaps closed.
2. Cover the box with construction paper. Draw and cut out a mouse hole from black paper and glue it in place. Draw and cut out a mouse and glue it in front of the door. Stick a tail of string under the mouse before the glue dries. Glue in place.
3. Add a sign that says "Mouse's House." Decorate with paper cutouts.
4. Place the doorstop by your front door.

Frosty Snowman Card

paper

1. Cut a piece of white paper 10 inches by 8 inches. Fold it in half to measure 5 inches by 4 inches.
2. Draw a snowman starting with the top of his hat at the fold line, and work down to the bottom of the paper.
3. Cut along the drawing of the snowman, but do not cut along the fold at the top of his hat.
4. Decorate with markers and cut paper and write a message inside.

Present Pin

cardboard ● fabric ● ribbon ● safety pin

1. Cover a small square of cardboard with fabric. Glue a ribbon around it to look like a package.
2. Glue a safety pin to the back.

Mini Elf

small and miniature-sized clay pots ● small wooden spool ● wiggle eyes ● small pompom

1. Paint a small and a miniature-sized clay pot. Let dry.
2. Glue a small wooden spool to the bottom of the small pot. Glue the miniature pot, upside down, on top of the spool. Glue wiggle eyes to the spool and draw a face. Glue a pompom at the top. Let dry.

Flower Angel Ornament

silk flower ● chenille stick ● wooden bead
● wireless chenille ● gold foil ● dental floss

1. Cut the wire stem of a silk flower about 2 inches from the base. Thread the leaves from the flower onto the stem for wings. Wrap a chenille stick around the stem to make arms.
2. Paint a face on a wooden bead and thread it onto the stem. Glue on wireless chenille for hair. Top the head with a circle of gold foil.
3. Bend the end of the wire stem into a circle. Add a loop of dental floss for a hanger.

Great Gift Tags

plastic-foam tray ● poster board ● wiggle eyes ● paper ● ribbon
● gingerbread-man cookie cutter ● felt ● buttons ● rickrack

1. To make the Santa, cut a circle from a plastic-foam tray. Add a hat from poster board. Add wiggle eyes and a paper mouth and nose. Cut pieces of ribbon, curl them around a pencil, and glue in place to make a beard.
2. With a hole punch, make a hole at the top of the hat and tie a loop of ribbon.
3. To make the "gingerbread" character, place a gingerbread-man cookie cutter on a piece of brown poster board and trace around it. Draw another line about ¼ inch from the traced outline and cut out the character on the outside line.
4. Place the cookie cutter on a piece of felt and trace around it. Cut out the design. Glue the felt piece on top of the poster board.
5. Add button eyes and a mouth and buttons down the body. Add rickrack for trim. Punch a hole at the top and add a loop of rickrack. Add a sign from poster board with the recipient's name on it. Use these gift tags as ornaments after the presents are opened.

Snowman-in-a-Bag

plastic-mesh vegetable bag ● cotton balls ● string ● ribbon ● cardboard ● 35mm plastic film canister ● paper ● button ● twigs

1. Fill a plastic-mesh vegetable bag with cotton balls. Gather at the top and tie a piece of string to hold the bag closed. Tie ribbon around the center, forming a head and a body.
2. To make a hat, cut and paint a small circle of cardboard. Then glue a black 35mm plastic film canister on top. Glue the hat in place.
3. Add paper eyes and a button nose. Cut out paper boots and glue in place. Add twigs for arms.

Glue-and-Glitter Star

chenille sticks ● plastic wrap ● glitter ● white glue ● star sticker

1. Make a star shape from glittery chenille sticks. Add a chenille-stick loop at one point.
2. Tape a piece of plastic wrap to a flat surface. Tape the chenille star down firmly to the plastic wrap, taping only the outside edges.
3. Mix glitter with white glue. Pour it into the star shape. Add a star sticker in the center. Sprinkle the glue with extra glitter and let dry. (It may take up to three days for the glue to dry completely.)
4. Carefully peel the star away from the plastic wrap. Hang the star by the loop on your holiday tree or in a window.

Cutout Gift Bag

paper bag ● paper ● self-adhesive reinforcement rings ● yarn

1. Before you decorate your bag, be sure your gift will fit inside.
2. Create a colorful scene by drawing and cutting out pieces of paper and gluing them to the front of the bag. Near the top, place two self-adhesive reinforcement rings. Use a hole punch to punch holes in the rings.
3. Close the bag. Punch through the front holes to the back of the bag. Add two self-adhesive rings to the back holes. Thread yarn through the holes to make a handle. Knot the ends.

Santa Scene

shoebox and lid ● construction paper ● white paper ● felt ● white cardboard

1. Cover the outside top and sides of a shoebox lid with construction paper. Cut a large hole in the top of the lid. Cover the outside of the shoebox with paper.
2. Inside the box, cut and glue white paper to the bottom and the two short sides. Cut and glue felt to one of the long sides to make a rug.
3. Lay the box on its side with the "rug" down. Draw and cut out a window and a door from paper and glue them on the back "wall."
4. Draw and cut out a Santa, Christmas tree, Rudolph, and other objects from white cardboard, leaving a tab at the bottom of each. Bend the tabs back and glue them inside Santa's house.
5. Glue the lid on the shoebox and place it on a table for decoration.

Pinecone Advent Wreath

craft sticks ● pinecones ● four small clay pots ● pine tree cuttings ● three purple candles ● pink candle ● white candle

1. Glue craft sticks together to make a circular wooden frame. Make it wide enough to lay pinecones and clay pots. Paint the frame brown. Let dry.
2. Place four clay pots on the frame, opposite one another. Add pinecones between the pots. Glue in place.
3. Push the pine tree cuttings between the pinecones and pots. Trim any excess from the cuttings.
4. Ask an adult to drip some wax into the pots to set the candles up straight.
5. Light a purple candle on the first, second, and fourth Sundays before Christmas. Light the pink one on the third Sunday. Light a white candle in the center on Christmas Day.

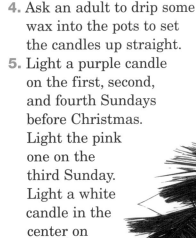

Pint-Sized Bell

pint-sized ice-cream container ● felt
● 2-inch plastic-foam ball ● yarn

1. Cover a pint-sized ice-cream container with felt and decorate with felt shapes.
2. Paint a 2-inch plastic-foam ball and let dry.
3. Poke a hole in the ball. Add glue in the hole and press one end of a piece of yarn into the hole. Tape the other end up inside the bell.
4. Glue on a loop of yarn for hanging.

Sleigh Card Caddy

cereal box ● poster board

1. Cut a section from a cereal box to make the holder. Cover the cutout section with red paint and let dry.
2. Draw runners for the sleigh on black poster board. Cut out the runners and glue them in place.
3. Fill the sleigh with holiday cards.

Sequin Christmas Tree

lightweight cardboard ● felt ● rickrack ● sequins ● ball ornament

1. Cover both sides of two pieces of lightweight cardboard with green felt. Draw and cut out a Christmas tree from a third piece of lightweight cardboard. Trace around the tree on each felt-covered board and cut them out.
2. On one tree, cut a slit in the center, beginning at the bottom and extending halfway up the tree. The slit should be slightly wider than the thickness of the cardboard. On the second tree, cut a slit in the center, beginning at the top and extending halfway down the tree.
3. Slip the two trees together to form a three-dimensional tree. Add glue at the seams and let dry.
4. Glue rickrack along the tree edges and let dry. Glue a variety of sequins to decorate the tree. Add a small ball ornament to the top.

Christmas "Kazoo"

gift wrap ● cardboard tube ● waxed paper ● hair band

1. Glue gift wrap around a 4½-inch cardboard tube.
2. Cut a round piece of waxed paper about 3½ inches in diameter. Place it over one end of the tube and hold it in place with a hair band.
3. Ask an adult to help you make three or four holes along the side of the tube with a pen or pencil.
4. Hum into the open end of the tube, and play the "kazoo" by covering and uncovering the holes with your fingers.

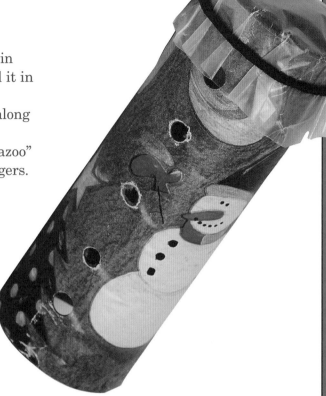

Horsing Around

old sock ● rags ● old broom handle ● heavy-duty tape ● large-eyed needle ● heavy thread ● ribbon ● silver buttons ● D rings ● jingle bells ● black buttons ● felt ● yarn

1. Stuff an old sock with rags. Put one end of an old broom handle into the sock as far as the heel. Stuff rags around the dowel, then tape the end of the sock to the handle.
2. Using a large-eyed needle and heavy thread, sew pieces of ribbon to make the bridle. (You may want to ask an adult to help you.) Sew on silver buttons for decoration. Sew two D rings to the ends of the ribbon near the mouth area for the bit ends. Sew each end of a long piece of ribbon to the D rings for reins. Sew jingle bells to the reins.
3. Sew on two black buttons for eyes, adding felt for details. Sew two felt ears and a blaze in place. Glue pieces of felt to make the nostrils, mouth, and tongue.
4. To make the mane, cut pieces of yarn 2 to 3 inches in length. Tie four to six pieces together in the middle with another piece of yarn. Sew the center of each bunch to the sock. Sew one bunch between the ears for the forelock.

17

Nutcracker Soldier

paper ● 12-inch cardboard tube ● red cording ● felt

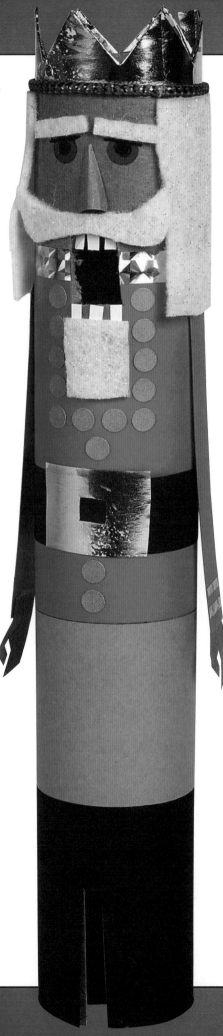

1. To make boots, cut a strip of black paper 2½ inches by 6 inches. Start at one end of a 12-inch cardboard tube and glue the paper around the tube. Cut a small section from the center.
2. Cut a strip of green paper 2 inches by 6 inches. Glue it above the boots to make pants. Cut a strip of red paper 1 inch by 6 inches. Glue it above the pants to make the bottom of the jacket.
3. Cut a strip of black paper 1 inch by 6 inches. Glue it above the jacket bottom for a belt. Cut a strip of red paper 2½ inches by 6 inches for the top of the jacket.
4. Cut a strip of gold paper ¼ inch by 6 inches. Glue it above the jacket for the collar. Cut and glue a strip of brown paper to cover the rest of the tube. Cut a strip of gold paper with saw-toothed edges and glue on as a crown. Trim with red cording.
5. Cut a hole for the mouth. Cut and glue strips of paper for arms. Add hands and paper trim. Add facial features from cut paper. Use pieces of felt for hair, eyebrows, and a beard.

Quilted Ornaments

foam paper ● fabric ● thread

1. Cut ornament shapes from foam paper.
2. Glue patches of scrap fabric onto the ornaments until they are completely covered.
3. Poke a hole at the top of each ornament and attach a thread-loop hanger.

Fluffy Snowman

poster board ● felt ● cotton balls ● fabric ● yarn

1. From poster board, cut the shape of a snowman wearing a hat. Cover the hat with glue and a piece of felt. Trim around the edges with scissors. Add felt decorations.
2. Glue cotton balls over the snowman's body. Glue pieces of felt for the face and buttons. Tie a strip of fabric around the neck for a scarf.
3. Use a small piece of yarn for a hanger, and glue it to the back of the snowman's hat.

Fruity Holiday Card

unsweetened fruit-drink powder ● water ● white nontoxic paint ● poster board

1. Mix unsweetened fruit-drink powder with a few drops of water.
2. Add white nontoxic paint and mix thoroughly.
3. Fold a piece of poster board in half to make a card, and paint on "fruity" holiday greetings. Let dry.
4. Send this to a friend. He or she can scratch the greeting and sniff the fruity aroma.

Reindeer Gift Box

cardboard box with lid ● paper ● buttons ● pompom ● four cellophane-wrapped candy canes ● ribbon

1. Cover the top and sides of a box lid with paper, or start with a decorative gift box.
2. Cut a head for the reindeer from paper. Glue on button-and-paper eyes and a red pompom nose. Arrange the cut-paper head and the cellophane-wrapped candy canes on the lid. Glue in place. Add a ribbon bow.

Macaroni Angel

wooden bead ● rigatoni ● seeds or barley
● elbow macaroni ● bow-tie macaroni
● paper ● string

1. To make the head and body, glue a wooden bead to one end of a piece of rigatoni. Let dry.
2. Glue poppy seeds, sesame seeds, or pieces of barley to the head for hair. Let dry.
3. Make arms by gluing a piece of elbow macaroni to each side of the body, with the curve facing forward as shown. Hold them in place until dry.
4. To make wings, glue the center of a piece of bow-tie macaroni to the upper back of the angel. Rest the angel on its back and let dry.
5. Paint the angel and let dry.
6. Glue a small piece of folded paper in place to look like a songbook.
7. Tie a loop of string around the neck to hang the ornament.

Evergreen Apple

ribbon ● apple
● evergreens
● wooden skewer

1. Tie a ribbon around a firm apple, the way you would tie a package, so that the apple can be hung.
2. Collect several different kinds of evergreens. Poke holes in the apple using a small wooden skewer. Push a piece of greenery firmly into each hole.
3. Continue until the apple is covered. The juice from the apple will keep the evergreens fresh. Hang the evergreen apple in a window or a doorway.

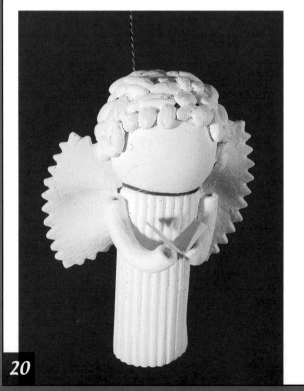

Peppermint Reindeer Pal

cellophane-wrapped candy cane ● wiggle eyes
● pompom ● chenille sticks ● string

1. Hold a cellophane-wrapped candy cane so that its curved top faces you. This part will be the reindeer's face. Keeping the wrapper on the candy cane, glue wiggle eyes and a red pompom to the reindeer's face.
2. Twist a chenille stick around the top of the head, and bend to create antlers. Add smaller pieces of chenille stick to make points on the antlers.
3. Tie a loop of string behind the antlers, and display the reindeer on your tree.

Santa Card Keeper

two large, heavy paper plates ● paper ● cotton balls ● cording

1. Cover the top of one large, heavy paper plate with red paint and let dry. Cut the other paper plate in half. With the bottom facing upward, paint the half plate in a skin color.
2. Place the half plate on top of the red plate. Staple around the edges, leaving the cut edge open.
3. For the face, cut out a paper mouth and eyes. Glue these to the plate half. Add cotton balls for the hair, the mustache, and the beard.
4. Add a cotton ball to the edge of the red plate to decorate the hat. Glue a loop of cording to the back for a hanger. Fill with cards.

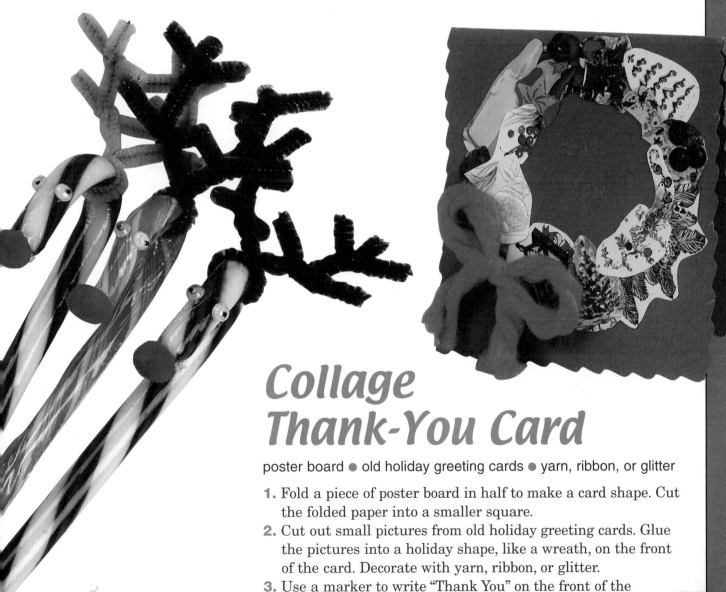

Collage Thank-You Card

poster board ● old holiday greeting cards ● yarn, ribbon, or glitter

1. Fold a piece of poster board in half to make a card shape. Cut the folded paper into a smaller square.
2. Cut out small pictures from old holiday greeting cards. Glue the pictures into a holiday shape, like a wreath, on the front of the card. Decorate with yarn, ribbon, or glitter.
3. Use a marker to write "Thank You" on the front of the card. Write a thank-you message inside.

Pot of Poinsettias

plastic-foam egg carton ● green chenille sticks ● green pompoms ● small plastic-foam ball ● small clay pot

1. Cut three cups from a plastic-foam egg carton. Trim the edges so that the cups have a spiky look. Paint each cup and let dry.
2. Cut green chenille sticks to various lengths and poke one end through each eggcup, bending the end slightly to hold it in place. Glue a green pompom to the center of each flower.
3. Firmly press a small plastic-foam ball into a small clay pot and trim. Paint the pot and the foam ball. Let dry.
4. Poke the chenille-stick stems into the foam.

Tissue Christmas Tree

poster board ● plastic-foam tray ● tissue paper ● paper plate

1. Cut a half circle from a piece of poster board. Place it on top of a plastic-foam tray to protect your work area. With a pencil, carefully poke holes through the half circle, about 1 inch apart. Discard the plastic-foam tray. Roll the half circle into a cone and tape it together.
2. Cut circles, about 3 inches in diameter, from tissue paper. Pinch the center of one of these circles into a point.
3. Squeeze some glue onto a small paper plate. Dip the point of the tissue into the glue. Starting from the bottom, insert the point of the tissue into one of the holes on the cone. Repeat until the tree is covered.
4. Add thin strips of tissue paper to the top.

Napkin Caddy

clear plastic detergent bottle ● felt ● lace ● sequins

1. On each side of a clear plastic detergent bottle, draw the shape shown, starting an inch up from the bottom. Cut along the dotted line and discard the top and side parts.
2. Cut and glue felt to cover the holder. Glue a lace ruffle around the bottom.
3. Cut and glue a felt tree to each side of the holder. Decorate with sequins.

Santa's Chimney Game

ribbon ● plastic berry basket ● plastic-foam ball
● wiggle eyes ● paper ● string

1. To make the chimney, cut strips of ribbon to weave in and out through sections of a plastic berry basket. Overlap the ends and glue together.
2. Paint and decorate a plastic-foam ball to look like Santa Claus. Use wiggle eyes and paper for the boots and mittens.
3. Attach string from the outside bottom of the basket to the Santa.
4. Hold the chimney in your hands and try to swing Santa into the chimney.

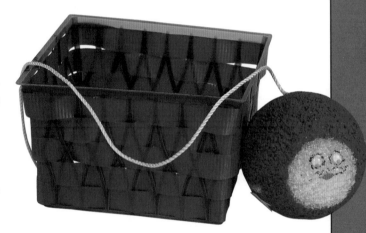

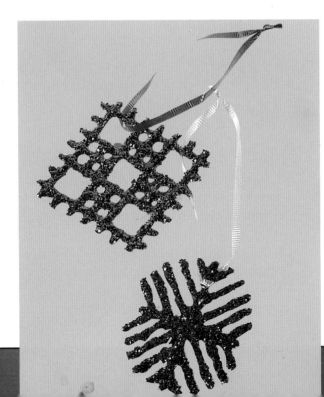

Sun Sparkler

plastic berry basket ● waxed paper
● glitter ● ribbon

1. Cut off the bottom of a plastic berry basket. Trim it to make a decorative shape, and place it on waxed paper.
2. Squeeze glue on the shape and add glitter. Let dry.
3. Turn the shape over and repeat step 2.
4. Use ribbon to hang your sun catcher in a window or on a tree.

Angel Flyer

construction paper ● paper doily ● cording
● wooden dowel

1. Draw and cut out two triangles from construction paper, making one a little smaller than the other. These will be the angel's dress. Draw and cut two sleeve shapes from paper. Use your scissors to round off the tip and to make a scallop design along the bottom of both triangles. Decorate the dress and sleeves with marker.

2. Cut two wing shapes from a paper doily. Glue the bottom of the wings in the center of the large triangle. Glue one end of a length of cording to the side of the triangle in between the wings.

3. Glue one of the sleeve shapes underneath the large triangle. Glue the smaller triangle over the first, matching all sides. Glue the other sleeve shape to the front of the dress.

4. Draw and cut a head, hands, and feet from paper. Color the tips of the feet to make shoes. Glue each foot underneath the dress. Glue the hands to the ends of the sleeves. Glue doily lace to the ends of the sleeves. Use marker to add hair, facial features, and a halo to the head shape. Glue the head shape in place.

5. Tie the loose end of the cording around a wooden dowel. Hold it to make your angel fly. Or omit the dowel and tie a loop in the cord. Hang your angel to decorate your home.

Cloth Wreath

wire clothes hanger ● fabric

1. Bend and shape the triangular section of a wire clothes hanger into a circle.
2. Cut fabric into strips about 9 inches long and ½ inch wide.
3. Tie the strips to the hanger. The more strips you use, the fuller the wreath will become.
4. Add a fabric bow.

24

Snowy Scene

heavy paper plate ● construction paper ● string

1. Paint the inside and outer edge of a heavy paper plate, making the background for a scene.
2. Cut a snowman, hat, and scarf from construction paper. Glue them onto the scene. Cut tiny pieces of white paper for the snowflakes and glue them around the outer edge of the plate.
3. Glue or tape a loop of string to the back for a hanger.

Two Gift Bows

ribbon ● cardboard ● wire

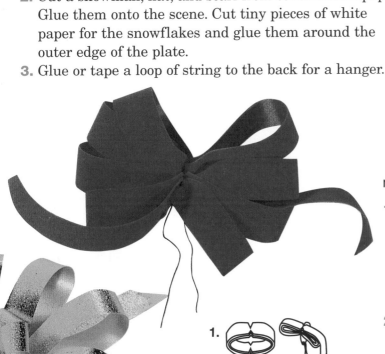

1. Wrap ribbon around a 2-inch-by-6-inch piece of cardboard. Cut notches at the center of both sides of the ribbon. Remove the cardboard. Twist wire around the notches. Spread out the ribbon, forming a bow.
2. Cut 8-inch strips of ribbon. Glue the ends of the strips together, making loops. Press and glue each loop in the center. Layer the loops on top of each other, and glue in place. Glue a small circle of ribbon in the center.

Holiday Tree Frog

cardboard ● spring-type clothespin ● wiggle eyes

1. Cut a frog shape from cardboard. Make the frog as long as a spring-type clothespin.
2. Glue a clothespin to the cardboard frog shape, leaving the gripping end sticking out.
3. Decorate your tree frog with brightly colored paint. Paint the clothespin red to look like a tongue. Let dry.
4. Glue on two large wiggle eyes.
5. Hang your colorful frog on your tree by clamping the clothespin over a branch.

Braided Scarf

60-inch-wide white fleece ● 60-inch-wide red fleece

1. Cut a 3-inch-by-60-inch length of white fleece. Cut two lengths of red fleece the same size.
2. Line up the ends of the three pieces of fleece and knot them together about 10 inches in from the end.
3. Close the knotted end in a drawer to hold the fleece in place. Braid the three pieces together loosely. (See diagram.)
4. Stop about 10 inches from the end and tie a knot.
5. Snip the ends into ½-inch-wide sections to make fringe.

Gift-Box Photo Frame

four large craft sticks ● poster board ● ribbon ● string ● photograph

1. Glue four large craft sticks together to form a square frame.
2. Cover the frame with a couple of coats of paint, letting each coat dry before adding another.
3. Cut four small squares from poster board. Decorate them with ribbon to look like packages. Glue one package to each corner.
4. Glue a string hanger to the back and let dry. Cut a photograph to fit the frame and tape it on the back.

Simple Scarf

60-inch-wide patterned fleece

1. Cut an 8-inch-by-60-inch length of fleece that has a pattern.
2. Snip the ends into ½-inch-wide sections to make fringe.
3. Tie a knot on each end of the scarf where the fringe meets the uncut fabric.

Frosty Hat Pompom

cardboard ● yarn ● needle and thread ● knit cap
● wiggle eyes ● felt

1. Cut a piece of cardboard 1½ inches by 2 inches. Wrap white yarn around it, as shown, about forty-five times, or more for a fuller pompom.
2. Carefully slip the yarn from the cardboard, and tie a piece of yarn tightly around and through the center of the loops. Cut through the loops at both ends. Fluff up the yarn.
3. Sew the white pompom to the cuff of a knit cap. Glue wiggle eyes in place. Add a felt hat and a mouth.

 Wrap yarn.

 Tie around and through loops.

 Cut loops.

Gingerbread Cutouts

light brown kraft paper

1. Cut a strip of light brown kraft paper about 18 inches by 3½ inches. Fold one end of the strip to make a rectangle about 2½ inches by 3½ inches. Fold the rest of the strip back and forth under the first rectangle, making each section the same size as the first.
2. On the first rectangle, draw a gingerbread character with hands touching the folds and the legs reaching the bottom of the paper.
3. Keeping the paper folded, cut out the character. Do not cut through the folded paper at the end of the hands. Unfold the paper.
4. The characters should be in a row, holding hands. Decorate them with markers.

Clay-Pot Reindeer Ornament

brown chenille sticks ● small clay pot ● wiggle eyes ● pompom ● ribbon

1. Cut and bend brown chenille sticks to look like antlers. Glue the antlers along the inside edge of a small clay pot so the tops stick up.
2. Glue on wiggle eyes and a pompom for the nose. Let dry.
3. Glue a piece of ribbon to the inside of the pot for a hanger.

Winter Blossom Card

construction paper ● glitter

1. Fold a sheet of construction paper to make a card.
2. Cut out petals from red paper. Glue the petals to the front of the card. Spread glue in the center and sprinkle on gold glitter. Let dry.
3. Shake off the excess glitter. Write a holiday message inside the card.

Holiday Message Center

heavy corrugated cardboard ● gift wrap ● ribbon ● cording

1. Cut two 12-inch squares from heavy corrugated cardboard. Glue or tape them together. Cover the cardboard with gift wrap, taping the extra paper on the back like a package.
2. Glue ribbon around the front and the back of the board. Let dry.
3. Ask an adult to help you poke two holes at the top of the board. Thread a piece of cording through the holes to hang the message board.

Fanfold Angel

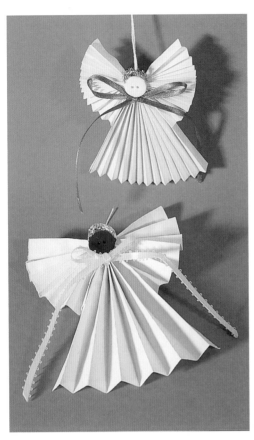

white paper ● strong thread ● paper clip ● chenille stick ● two-hole button ● ribbon ● string

1. Cut two pieces of white paper of equal size. The larger angel in the picture was made with 4-inch-by-5½-inch strips; the smaller angel was made with 3-inch-by-5½-inch strips.
2. Fanfold each strip across the longer side.
3. Pinch one folded strip together in the middle to make an hourglass shape, and pinch the second strip at the top to make a fan shape. Use a small piece of strong thread to hold each piece in place.
4. Place the hourglass shape above the fan shape so that the pinched parts of the two pieces touch, forming a T shape. Glue the bottom edge of the wings to the sides of the angel. Use a paper clip to hold them in place while the glue dries.
5. To form a halo, cut a small piece of silver chenille stick. Glue the edges of the halo to a two-hole button, then glue the button to the angel.
6. Glue a ribbon under the button head to decorate, then add a string for a hanger.

Kris Kringle Mask

large paper bag ● construction paper

1. Measure about 4 inches from the opening of a large paper bag, and cut around the entire bag.
2. For a hat, fold down the top corners of a piece of construction paper to make a triangle shape. Tape the wide base to the top front of the bag. Do the same on the back of the bag. Tape the side triangles together. Trim to fit.
3. Put the bag on your head. Using a crayon, have a friend carefully mark where the eyes should be. Remove the bag. Cut out a large opening for the eyes.
4. Cut out a white paper beard and mustache to fit the front of the bag. Cut slits into the bottom and sides of the paper. Curl the edges of the beard by rolling them around a pencil. Glue in place. Cut out hair and eyebrows and do the same. Cut out a mouth shape from the bag.
5. Wear a red sweatshirt when you put on the mask.

Christmas Candle

lid from pint-sized ice-cream container ● felt ● cardboard tube ● cardboard ● chenille stick

1. Cover a pint-sized ice-cream container lid with felt. Make a loop with two felt strips glued together. Glue the loop to the side.
2. Cut a cardboard tube down to 3½ inches. Cover it with felt, and glue it to the lid. Add felt details.
3. Cut a cardboard circle to fit the top of the candle. Cover the circle with felt. Poke a piece of chenille stick through the circle for a wick. Cover it with a felt flame and glue the circle to the top of the candle.

Sweet Scents

cinnamon ● bowl ● measuring spoons ● applesauce ● waxed paper ● cookie cutter ● table knife ● paper plate ● ribbon

1. Put ¼ cup of cinnamon in a bowl. Stir in 4 tablespoons of applesauce. The mixture should feel like cookie dough. If it's too sticky, add more cinnamon. If it's too dry, add more applesauce.
2. On waxed paper, flatten the dough with your hand. Use a cookie cutter to make shapes, or use a table knife to create your own cutouts.
3. Place the shapes on a paper plate. Use a pencil to make a hole in the top of each shape.
4. Let dry for about a week.
5. Tie ribbon through each hole to hang.

Jingle-Bell Necklace

wooden spools ● fabric ● jingle bells ● cording ● tiny bells

1. Place wooden-spool ends on fabric and trace around them with a pencil. Cut out the circles of fabric and glue them on the spool ends. Cut a small X through the fabric and center holes of each spool.
2. Glue fabric around the spools and let dry.
3. Thread the spools and jingle bells on a piece of cording long enough to hang loosely around your neck. Make a knot on either side of the spools and through the bells so they stay put. Add tiny bells at the ends.

Santa Puppet

paper ● cardboard oatmeal container ● felt
● rubber band ● cotton balls ● pompom

1. Cut a piece of paper to fit around a cardboard oatmeal container. Glue the paper in place. Discard the lid.
2. To make the hat, cut out a circle of red felt larger in diameter than the container. Turn the container upside down so the bottom faces upward. Spread glue around the outside bottom edge. Place the edge of the felt in the glue, gathering the felt together if needed. Hold in place with a rubber band and let dry.
3. Glue a cotton ball to the top of the hat, and add some around the bottom. Make eyes and a mouth from paper. Attach them with glue. Add cotton balls for hair, a beard, eyebrows, and a mustache. Glue on a pompom nose.
4. Place your arm and hand inside the container to move your puppet.

Candy-Cane Lane

floral foam block ● gift wrap ● ribbon
● cellophane-wrapped candy canes
● cotton balls ● paper

1. Cover a floral foam block with gift wrap. Tape two pieces of ribbon around the sides for decoration.
2. With a pencil, gently poke holes in various places on the foam block. Insert cellophane-wrapped candy canes in the holes.
3. To make snowmen, glue two cotton balls together. Add paper eyes, a mouth, and a hat to each one. Glue them near the candy canes.
4. Place the decoration on a table. Replace the candy canes as they are eaten.

Matching Mitten Game and Ornaments

cardboard ● red and white felt
● spring-type clothespins

1. Make a simple mitten pattern from cardboard. Use the pattern to cut eight mittens from red felt.
2. Cut four pairs of matching holiday shapes from white felt. Glue one shape to each mitten.
3. To play, place the mittens plain-side up. Turn the mittens over two at a time. If the shapes match, keep the mittens. If not, flip them back over. Keep trying until you have matched them all. (To make the game more challenging, make more pairs of mittens with different shapes.)
4. When you finish playing, hang the mittens on your Christmas tree using spring-type clothespins.

Ribbon Organizer

felt ● cardboard tube ● cardboard

1. For the body, cut a piece of gray felt and glue it around a cardboard tube. Cut a head and ear shapes from cardboard. Cover both sides with felt. Glue the head to one end of the tube with the ears in between. Let dry.
2. Draw and cut legs and feet from the cardboard. Cover both sides with felt. Glue them in place.
3. For the tail, cut a long, thin piece of felt and glue it at the end of the tube.
4. Wrap loose ribbon around the body of the mouse and tape the ends securely until needed.

Rectangle Santa

construction paper ● cotton balls

1. Cut two large and two small rectangles from red construction paper.
2. Glue or staple these together so that the two larger rectangles hang down for Santa's legs and the smaller rectangles stick out on each side for his arms.
3. Cut a head and hands from construction paper and attach them in place. Give Santa a red hat and black boots and belt.
4. Draw his face, then give him a cotton-ball beard. Trim his suit and hat with cotton balls.

Potato-Print Press

paper bag ● potato ● paper ● table knife ● ribbon

1. Before you decorate your bag, be sure your gift will fit inside.
2. Wash and dry a potato half. Draw a simple design on a piece of paper and cut it out. Place the design on the cut side of the potato. Using a table knife, cut away the area around the design, leaving the design about a ½ inch above the rest of the potato.
3. Paint the potato design and press it onto the paper bag. Repeat the painting and printing. Let the paint dry before you put the gift inside.
4. Fold over the top of the bag, and punch two holes through the flap. Thread a ribbon through and tie it into a bow.

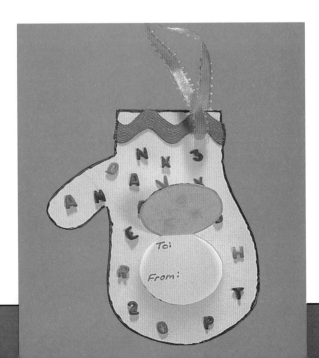

Peek-a-Boo Tag

construction paper ● white paper ● decorative trims ● ribbon

1. Cut out a holiday shape from construction paper. Cut a flap in the center.
2. Glue a piece of white paper to the back of the shape so that the white paper shows through the window.
3. Decorate the shape, then punch a hole at the top. Use ribbon to turn it into a gift tag.
4. Open the flap and write a message on the white paper.

Peppermint Sleigh

cardboard egg carton ● red and white chenille sticks ● pliers ● cotton ● cellophane-wrapped peppermint candies

1. Cut one cup from a cardboard egg carton, leaving one side a little taller than the other. The shorter side will be the front of your sleigh. Paint red and white stripes on the outside of the cup. Let dry.
2. Twist a red chenille stick together with a white one. Create two of these. Glue them to the bottom of the cup. Make sure a short piece extends out the front of the sleigh and a longer piece extends up the back. Glue the chenille-stick twists to the back of the sleigh. Use pliers to roll the ends.
3. Glue a little cotton into the sleigh for snow.
4. Make several sleighs and fill them with cellophane-wrapped peppermint candies. Add them to your holiday dinner table so each guest will have a take-home treat.

Mr. Claus Tissue Dispenser

red tissue paper ● unopened box of facial tissues ● cotton ball ● white paper ● construction paper

1. Use a double-folded sheet of red tissue paper that is long enough to cover an unopened box of facial tissues and to extend beyond it for the hat as shown. Cover three sides. Cover the fourth side only up to the slot through which the facial tissue will be removed. This will be the back.
2. Gather the hat into a point and staple. Glue on a cotton ball.
3. For the beard, cut a piece of white paper to cover the front and to overlap about 1½ inches on each side. Scallop the bottom with scissors and glue in place. For the face, cut a half circle from skin-colored construction paper. Glue it about 1 inch from the top of the box. Add eyes, eyebrows, and a mouth from paper.
4. Glue a paper band around the base of the hat and coat and add a black belt and white buckle.

Sock-Puppet Reindeer

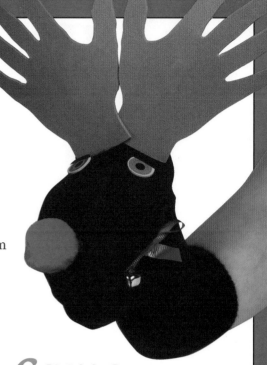

foam paper ● spring-type clothespins
● old sock ● paper ● pompom ● ribbon ● bell

1. To make the antlers, trace around your hands on foam paper and cut them out. Glue each to a spring-type clothespin.
2. Lay an old sock on a table. Cut out eyes from paper and foam paper. Glue them to the bottom of the sock. Add a red pompom for a nose.
3. Glue a ribbon with a bell on the leg area of the sock. Place your hand inside the sock, and clip on the antlers at the heel of the sock.

Tree Tally Game

two white poster boards ● yardstick ● plastic lids

1. Tape two white poster boards together end to end on one side. Turn the boards over. Using a yardstick and a pencil, draw a tree shape, including its trunk.
2. Divide the tree into sections using a black marker. Draw a number in each section. Color the tree green, leaving the numbers white. Color the trunk brown.
3. Place the tree on the floor. Give each player a turn at throwing three plastic lids onto the playing board. Total each player's score after three throws. See who can get the highest number of points.

Santa Treat Tray

9-inch-round aluminum foil pan ● gift wrap
● clear self-adhesive paper ● ribbon ● metal fastener ● paper

1. Trace around the outside of a 9-inch-round aluminum foil pan on a piece of gift wrap and a piece of clear self-adhesive paper. Cut out the circles.
2. First glue the gift-wrap circle in the pan. Then you may want to ask an adult to help you separate the adhesive paper from its backing and place the adhesive-paper circle on top of the gift wrap.
3. Glue a piece of ribbon around the outer edge of the pan. Add a ribbon bow with a metal fastener. Attach a note that says "For Santa" on the edge.
4. Fill the pan with cookies and a glass of milk for Santa on Christmas Eve.

35

Gingerbread Boy

corrugated cardboard ● brown construction paper
● white cording ● foam paper

1. Draw a gingerbread boy shape on corrugated cardboard. Cut it out.
2. Wrap brown construction paper around the shape. Glue it to the back.
3. Glue white cording around the edges to look as if he is trimmed with frosting.
4. Punch circles of foam paper to make buttons and eyes. Glue them in place. Add cording for a mouth.
5. Glue cording on the back for a hanger.

Santa's Express

individual-sized cereal boxes ● construction paper
● plastic caps ● foam paper ● string

1. Close the flaps of empty individual-sized cereal boxes with tape. Cover with glue and construction paper.
2. Decorate the cars and caboose with paper windows. Draw children looking out. Add signs that say "Santa." Decorate the engine with paper windows. Add the engineers.
3. Glue various types of plastic caps to the engine and caboose. Cut out foam-paper wheels and glue them to the train.
4. Attach the cars together with pieces of string and glue.

Film-Can Ornament

old holiday greeting cards
● 35mm plastic film canister ● ribbon

1. Cut out pictures from old holiday greeting cards. Trim them to the size of a 35mm plastic film canister.
2. Glue the pictures to the canister.
3. To make the hanger, glue a piece of ribbon underneath the lid. When dry, replace the lid on the canister. Trim with ribbon.

Christmas Countdown Keeper

poster board ● construction paper ● white glue ● chalk

1. Draw a snowman (or another design) on poster board and cut it out.
2. Cut out a heart from black construction paper. Cut out a bigger heart from paper of any color.
3. Glue the big heart on the snowman. Glue the black heart on top. Paint white glue on the black heart. Let dry.
4. Cut out a hat and scarf from paper and glue them on. Use markers to draw a face. Write "Christmas Countdown!"
5. On the black heart, use chalk to write the number of days left until the holiday. To change the number, erase it with a dry cloth.

Sock Wreath

old tube sock ● cotton ● yarn ● construction paper

1. Stuff an old tube sock with cotton. Tie the ends together with yarn to form a wreath.
2. Paint and let dry. Paint on a design and let dry.
3. Cut out a bow from construction paper and glue it onto the wreath.

Fabric Patch Ornament

fabric ● 3-inch plastic-foam ball ● table knife ● ribbon ● straight pin

1. Cut small pieces of fabric in different shapes. Place one piece on a 3-inch plastic-foam ball. Gently press the corners of the fabric into the ball with a table knife.
2. To place the second piece of fabric, overlap one edge of the first piece of fabric, and press in. Continue until the entire ball is covered.
3. Fold a piece of ribbon so the ends overlap. Stick a straight pin through the overlap, and pin the ribbon to the quilted ball for hanging.

Gift Tower

heavy cardboard ● felt ● cardboard tube ● plastic-foam block ● gift wrap ● ribbon

1. Cut one 10-inch-by-2½-inch cardboard strip for the bottom, one 7-inch-by-2½-inch strip for the middle, and one 4-inch-by-2½-inch strip for the top, and cover them with green felt.
2. Cut three 2½-inch pieces from a cardboard tube and cover with green felt. Cut a 3½-inch section from a cardboard tube and cover with brown felt to make a stand.
3. Glue two green tube sections between the bottom and middle strips and the other green section between the middle and top strips. Space these evenly so you have room to fit the gift packages.
4. Glue the tower onto the brown felt stand.
5. Cut six cubes from a plastic-foam block. Decorate them with gift wrap and ribbon to look like gifts. Glue them to the tower.

Doorknob Decoration

felt ● lightweight cardboard ● sequins ● glitter

1. Cut out a 4-inch circle from a piece of red felt and lightweight cardboard. Glue them together.
2. Make a dot in the center of the cardboard. Draw an X through the dot. Cut along the lines of the X.
3. Cut several holly leaves from green felt, and cut berries from red felt. Glue the leaves around the outside edge of the circle, then add the berries. Glue on sequins and glitter.
4. Slip the wreath over a doorknob.

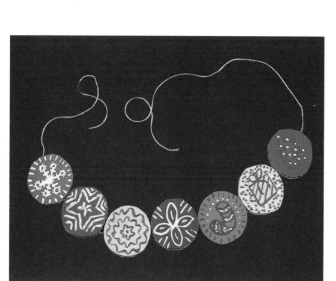

Colorful Chain

corrugated cardboard ● long sewing needle ● string

1. Cut several 2½-inch circles from corrugated cardboard. Paint the circles, making designs on both sides.
2. When dry, hold them together by threading a long sewing needle with string through the corrugated sections of the cardboard.
3. Hang the chain or tie it to your tree.

Christmas-Bell Card

white paper ● ribbon ● construction paper

1. Cut two pieces of white paper about 3 inches square. Fold them in half. Draw a half bell at the folded edge. Cut out the two bells.
2. Using a hole punch, hold the bells together and punch a hole at the top of the bells. Tie the bells together with ribbon. Write a message on the top bell.
3. Cut a piece of construction paper 9 inches by 5 inches. Fold it in half to 4½ inches by 5 inches.
4. Glue the back of the bottom bell to the center of the card. Glue only the fold line of the top bell to the bottom bell, making a three-dimensional effect.

Snowflakes

newspaper ● white glue ● disposable container
● yarn ● large plastic lid ● glitter ● thread

1. Cover your work space with newspaper. Squeeze white glue into a disposable container. Dip pieces of yarn in the glue. Press the yarn through your fingers to remove excess glue.
2. Place the glue-covered yarn on a large plastic lid, creating snowflake shapes. Let dry.
3. Peel the shapes away from the lid. Brush a little glue on each snowflake and sprinkle them with glitter. Let dry.
4. Add a thread-loop hanger.

Holly Napkin Rings

empty adhesive-tape rings ● ribbon ● felt

1. Cover the outside of empty adhesive-tape rings with glue and ribbon.
2. Cut holly leaves and berries from felt. Glue them to the rings.
3. Place a napkin in each ring for your dinner guests.

Holiday Planter

clay flowerpot and base
● high-gloss water-based crystal-clear glaze

1. Paint a clay flowerpot and base and let dry. Paint on a holiday design.
2. When dry, ask an adult to help you cover the flowerpot and base with a clear glaze, following the package directions.

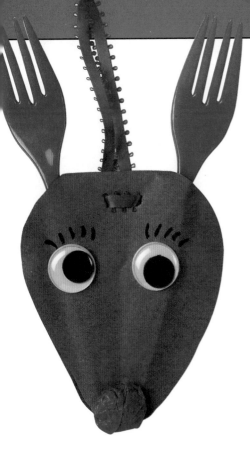

Fork-Antler Reindeer

construction paper ● plastic forks ● wiggle eyes ● tissue paper ● ribbon

1. Fold a piece of brown construction paper in half. Trace a simple reindeer head onto the paper so the top is along the fold. Cut it out, leaving the fold intact.
2. Spread glue along the handles of two plastic forks. Place them inside the head so they stick out the top when the paper is folded. Add glue around the edge of the head and fold the paper closed.
3. Add wiggle eyes and a crushed tissue-paper nose. Draw eyelashes.
4. Add ribbon for a hanger and place your reindeer on the tree.

Christmas Elf

craft stick ● chenille sticks ● wiggle eyes ● pompom

1. Break a craft stick in half. Trim the rough edge.
2. Twist green and red chenille sticks together to make a striped chenille stick. Cut it in half.
3. Lay the striped chenille-stick halves together on top of one craft-stick half. (See Diagram 1.)
4. Hold the striped chenille sticks firmly in place. Wrap a green chenille stick evenly around the craft stick until the stick is half-covered. (See Diagram 2.)
5. Fold out the tops of the striped chenille sticks to make arms, and wrap the craft stick a few more times. Leave part of the craft stick showing (for the head). Glue on wiggle eyes.
6. Separate the bottoms of the striped chenille sticks to make legs, and bend the ends for feet.
7. Twist a small piece of red or green chenille stick around the head for a hat and another at the neck for a scarf. Glue a tiny red pompom atop the hat. Let dry.

Diagram 1   Diagram 2

Tissue Angel

tissue paper ● craft stick ● chenille stick
● large wooden bead ● wiggle eyes

1. Fold blue tissue paper into a fan and glue it to a craft stick held straight up, covering the stick. Fold yellow tissue paper into a fan and glue it horizontally to the back of the craft stick for the wings. Let dry.
2. Bend a chenille stick and glue it to the top of the craft stick so that it forms a halo. Glue on a large wooden bead and wiggle eyes. Let dry.
3. Draw a face on the angel.

Mrs. Claus Box Puppet

individual-sized cereal box ● construction paper ● felt ● cotton balls
● pompom ● craft eyeglasses ● large chenille stick

1. Secure the top of an individual-sized cereal box with tape. Cover the box with construction paper.
2. Cut through the box about 1 inch from the bottom, leaving the back uncut. Cut and glue paper and felt features for the face, using the cut at the center as the mouth. Add cotton balls for hair, a pompom nose, and craft eyeglasses.
3. Make a hat from felt and a large chenille stick. Glue the hat in place.
4. Cut two small holes through the back, one at the top for your index finger and one at the bottom for your thumb to fit into. Work the puppet with your fingers inside the holes.

Hand-Stamped Wrapping Paper

foam paper ● film canisters ● unused pencil ● brown kraft paper
● white paper

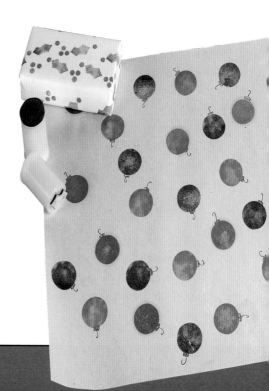

1. Cut out the shape of a holly leaf from foam paper and glue it to the bottom of a film canister to make a stamp.
2. Design wrapping paper with paint and your stamp. Add holly berries using the eraser of an unused pencil as a stamp. Make large sheets of wrapping paper with brown kraft paper and smaller sheets with white paper.
3. Glue a circle of foam paper to the bottom of another film canister. Use it as a stamp to make Christmas ornaments. Add details with a pen and marker.

Christmas-Tree Skirt

fabric

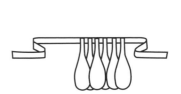

1. Draw and cut out a teardrop-shaped pattern on an 18-inch-by-7-inch piece of paper.
2. Place the pattern on a piece of fabric 2 yards wide and 20 inches long. Pin to hold. Ask an adult to help you cut around the pattern, using sewing scissors or a pair of pinking shears for a saw-toothed edge. Cut ten to twelve teardrop shapes.
3. Cut a strip of fabric about 3½ inches wide and 2 yards long. Staple the narrow end of one teardrop shape to the center of the strip of cloth. Continue to staple the teardrops on either side of the center, overlapping each teardrop halfway.
4. Place the skirt around the base of your tree, and tie the ends of the strip into a bow.

Jar Candleholder

two baby-food jars ● sand ● masking tape ● red cording ● foam paper ● construction paper ● candle

1. Fill one baby-food jar with sand and attach the lid.
2. Starting at the edge of the lid, wrap masking tape around the jar until it is completely covered. (Do not cover the top or the bottom of the jar.) Cover the other jar, without a lid, in the same way. Paint the jars. Let dry.
3. Glue the two jars together, keeping the one filled with sand on the bottom.
4. Spread glue around the top and middle of the holder. Wrap red cording around these sections, pressing the cording into the glue. Decorate with a poinsettia flower made from foam paper and punched-paper dots.
5. Place a candle in the jar, and pour sand around it to hold it in place.

Santa's Reindeer

construction paper

1. Cut a strip of construction paper about 16 inches long and 3½ inches wide. Fold it in half three times.
2. With the folds at the sides, draw a reindeer's head. Bring the tip of the nose and two antlers to the edge of the right side, and two antlers to the edge of the left side as shown in the diagram.
3. Keeping the paper folded, cut out the reindeer. Do not cut on the fold. Open the chain. Color the noses and draw the eyes.

Christmas Notes

old holiday greeting card
● cardboard ● white paper

1. Cut around a picture from an old holiday greeting card to make the front of the note pad.
2. Place the picture on a piece of cardboard and trace around it. Cut out the cardboard.
3. Stack some sheets of white paper. Place the picture on the top sheet and trace around the picture. Holding the sheets of paper together, cut out the shape.
4. Place the sheets of paper between the picture and the cardboard. Staple together at the top.

Felt Candle Card

white poster board
● paper ● felt

1. Fold a piece of white poster board to form a card. Cut and glue a piece of paper on the front of the card.
2. Cut 1-inch-square pieces of felt. Cut these into smaller pieces and glue them to the front of the card, creating a candle shape.
3. Add a paper base and flame to the candle. Write a greeting inside.

Holiday Card Wreath

old holiday greeting cards ● ribbon ● yarn

1. On the back of a card, draw and cut out a 2-inch-by-4-inch rectangle for a pattern.
2. Gather old holiday greeting cards. Trace around the pattern onto the fronts of about seventeen cards.
3. Cut out the rectangles. Arrange them in a circle, overlapping the edges. Glue them together where they overlap.
4. Make a bow from ribbon and glue it on. Tape a yarn loop on the back as a hanger.

Jingle-Bell Ring

wide cardboard ring ● glitter ● waxed paper ● cording ● jingle bell ● ribbon

1. Paint a wide cardboard ring. (Use the empty cardboard ring from a roll of wide tape, or cut a ring-shaped piece from a large empty roll of gift wrap.) Let dry.
2. Spread glue around both edges of the ring. Pour a little glitter onto a piece of waxed paper and press the edges into the glitter. Let dry.
3. Cut a short length of cording and thread it through the top of a jingle bell. Knot the ends together. Glue the knot to the inside of the ring.
4. Make a loop and bow of ribbon. Glue the bottom of the loop to the outside of the ring, making sure the bell hangs down.
5. Hang your decoration on your Christmas tree or in your home.

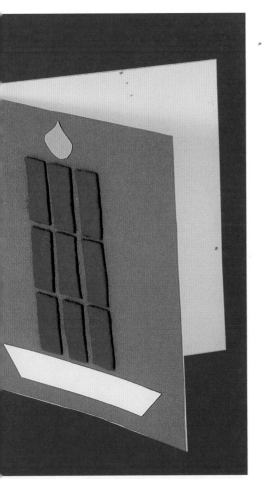

Christmas Mouse Treat Container

nut can and lid ● felt ● large and small pompoms ● chenille sticks ● cotton balls ● yarn ● newspaper

1. Cover a nut can with felt. Glue felt to the top of the lid.
2. Glue on felt facial features, a pompom nose, and chenille-stick whiskers. For each ear, cut two circles of felt, stuff cotton balls in between them, and glue them together. Add pink felt trim. Glue the ears to the sides of the can.
3. Braid about six strands of yarn together and glue it on for a tail. (See diagram.)
4. Cut out a 6-inch-by-12-inch piece of felt, glue the short sides together, and fold up a cuff on one of the long sides. Cut fringe along the top and tie with yarn. Add felt holly and a pompom berry. Stuff the hat with crumpled newspaper, and glue the hat to the top of the lid.

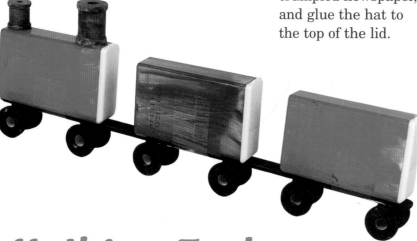

Holiday Train

craft sticks ● small wooden spools ● mint containers

1. Paint two craft sticks and six small wooden spools black. Paint two more spools green. Let dry.
2. Paint three mint containers. Let dry.
3. Tape the craft sticks underneath the containers with the middle container overlapping both craft sticks. Glue the green spools to the top of the first container to create the engine. Let dry.
4. Glue the black spools underneath the sticks. Let dry.

Chain of Holly

green and red construction paper

1. Fold a 3-inch-by-4-inch piece of green construction paper in half, the long way. Draw half of a double holly leaf and cut it out along the dotted lines as shown.
2. Fold back the center of the leaf at the solid line. Cut several leaves. Hook each leaf around the next one to make a chain.
3. Cut and glue red paper berries along the holly.

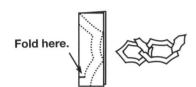

Fold here.

Santa Christmas-Card Bag

construction paper

- 6-inch-by-12-inch brown paper bag
- cotton balls
- self-adhesive reinforcement rings
- ribbon

1. Cut and glue red construction paper to cover the lower three-fourths of a 6-inch-by-12-inch brown paper bag.
2. Cut a 4-inch circle of paper for the face and a red triangle for the hat. Glue in place. Glue on cotton balls to trim the hat.
3. Add eyes and a mouth from paper. Glue on cotton balls for eyebrows, a mustache, and a beard. Glue paper mittens, a belt, and boots in place. Trim the coat with cotton balls.
4. On the back of the bag near the top, place two self-adhesive reinforcement rings about 2 inches apart. Make a hole through the centers, and string a ribbon through for hanging.

Foam-Tree Card

foam paper ● poster board ● construction paper

1. Draw a tree on foam paper, and cut it out.
2. Glue the tree to the front of a folded piece of poster board.
3. Glue construction-paper dots to the tree. Add a trunk and a star from paper.

Stained-Glass Angel

black construction paper ● waxed paper
● water ● tissue paper ● yarn

1. Cut ¼-inch strips of black construction paper. Arrange them on a piece of waxed paper, snipping as necessary, to create the outline of an angel. Glue the strips together.
2. Mix a small amount of glue with some water. Cut 1-inch squares of colored tissue paper. Pick a different color for each section of your angel, then place the tissue squares in layers in each section. Using fingers dipped in the glue-and-water mixture, smooth each piece. Add several layers for strength and brightness. Let dry.
3. Carefully peel the angel off the waxed paper. Glue a yarn loop to the back and hang in a sunny window.

Cardboard-Tube Wreath

cardboard ● cardboard tubes ● beads
● construction paper ● tissue ● string

1. To make the base, ask an adult to help you cut a 7-inch-wide circle from cardboard. Measure 2 inches from the outer edge and draw a smaller circle inside. Cut out a 3-inch circle from the center.
2. Cut off ten 1-inch rings from cardboard tubes. Cut a zigzag or scalloped edge on one side of each ring. Glue the flat side of the rings onto the base of the wreath and let dry.
3. Paint the rings and the base green and let them dry. Add another coat of paint.
4. Add beads and construction-paper holly leaves to the edge of the wreath. Wad up some tissue and glue it in one of the rings, filling it. Glue a paper bow on top of the tissue. Add a loop of string to the back.

Felt Christmas Ball

felt ● yarn ● cotton ● sequins

1. Draw and cut out two identical circles from felt.
2. Cut a length of yarn, fold it in half, and place the ends on one circle. Lay cotton on top, then the other felt circle, and glue the circles together.
3. Glue sequins on both sides to decorate.

Holiday Photo Frame

lightweight cardboard ● gift wrap ● photograph

1. Cut two rectangular pieces of lightweight cardboard the same size, one for the back section and one for the front. Cut out from the front section an area large enough to fit a photograph.
2. Cover the pieces of cardboard with gift wrap and tape down. To cut out the section for the photo, cut an X from corner to corner and fold back the paper. Trim and then glue the four flaps.
3. Place a photo in the opening, and tape it to the back of the front section. Glue the two cardboard sections together.
4. Cut a small piece of cardboard, and cover it with gift wrap. Glue the cardboard in the middle of the back of the frame so it stands up.

Candy-Cane Cutout

poster board ● waxed paper ● glitter
● ribbon ● jingle bell ● string

1. Draw a candy cane on white poster board. Cut out the shape, and punch a hole in the top.
2. Use markers to draw stripes.
3. Set the candy cane on a piece of waxed paper. Spread glue around the edges of the candy cane, then sprinkle glitter on the glue. Let dry.
4. Tie a ribbon around the candy cane, and attach a jingle bell.
5. To hang your candy cane or to attach it to a gift, tie a piece of string through the hole in the top.

Cookie-Cutter Ornament

string ● bell ● cookie cutter ● ribbon

1. Tie one end of a piece of string to a small bell. Tie the other end to a cookie cutter so the small bell hangs in the center.
2. Glue ribbon to the outside of the cookie cutter, making a loop at the top for a hanger. Let dry.

Doily Decoration

waxed paper ● craft sticks ● paper doily ● dental floss

1. Place waxed paper on your work surface. Paint three craft sticks. Let dry between two coats of paint.
2. Glue the sticks together in the centers, one on top of the other. Place a piece of waxed paper and a heavy object on top of the sticks to press them together. Let dry.
3. Decorate with pieces cut from a white paper doily. Add a loop of dental floss for a hanger.

Santa Candy Caddy

poster board ● white paper ● cardboard egg carton

1. Cut a large half circle, about 12 inches across, from red poster board. Cut a smaller half circle, about 6 inches across. Form each into a cone and tape the ends.
2. Cut a piece of white paper for the face. Fringe and curl the edges of the paper to make a beard, and add facial features. Glue the face to the larger cone.
3. To make a tassel, poke some thin white strips of paper through the top of the small cone, and glue them in place. Glue the small cone on top of the larger one.
4. Cut and paint cups from a cardboard egg carton. When dry, glue them around the bottom of the Santa. Fill with treats.

Holiday Puzzle

old holiday greeting card ● poster board
● envelope

1. Choose an old holiday greeting card that has a festive scene on it. Cut a piece of poster board the same size as the greeting card.
2. Spread a thin layer of glue on the poster board and glue the greeting card to it. Let dry.
3. On the back of the poster board, draw a pattern for the puzzle pieces, dividing the board into about twelve pieces. Carefully cut along the lines of the pattern.
4. Put the puzzle pieces in an envelope and give it to a friend.

Cone Stack Tree

green paper ● cotton swab

1. Draw and cut two half circles from green paper. Make one a little smaller than the other.
2. Roll each half circle into a cone shape and tape the ends to secure. Use scissors to snip fringe around the bottom of each cone. Use your fingers to curl the fringe upward.
3. Glue the smaller cone over the top of the larger cone to make a tree.
4. To decorate, dab paint onto the cone tree with a cotton swab.

51

Candy-Cane Heart

cellophane-wrapped candy canes ● ribbon

1. Tape together two cellophane-wrapped candy canes so that they form a heart shape.
2. Tie ribbon pieces to the top V of the heart. With an adult's help, use scissors to curl the ribbon ends.
3. For a hanger, tie on a ribbon loop.

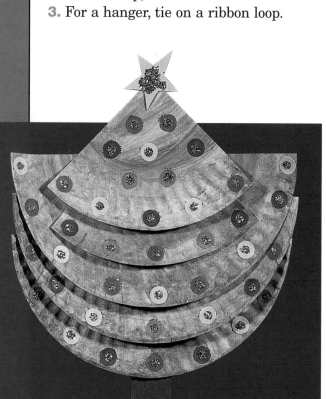

Paper-Plate Tree

two 9-inch paper plates ● poster board ● construction paper ● self-adhesive reinforcement rings ● glitter ● yarn

1. Paint two 9-inch white paper plates green. Cut both plates in half, then cut one section in half again.
2. On poster board, arrange the plate pieces to form a tree shape, and glue in place. Attach a brown construction-paper tree trunk.
3. Color self-adhesive reinforcement rings with markers. Place the rings on the tree. Drop glue inside each hole, and sprinkle it with glitter.
4. Add a glittery star to the top of the tree. Glue yarn to the back for a hanger.

Clothespin Reindeer

spring-type clothespins ● craft stick ● pompom ● wiggle eyes ● yarn

1. Glue one spring-type clothespin on one end of a craft stick and another about 1 inch in from the other end. Glue on a third clothespin for the head and antlers. Paint the reindeer brown. Let dry.
2. Glue on a red pompom nose and wiggle eyes. Let dry.
3. Tie a piece of red yarn into a bow around the neck.

Bell Wreath

cardboard ● green yarn
● plastic-foam trays ● glitter ● ribbon

1. To make a wreath, cut a doughnut shape from cardboard about 9 inches in diameter. Tape the starting end of a ball of green yarn to the cardboard. Wrap the yarn around the cardboard until it is covered. Tuck the finished end under the wrapped yarn.
2. Draw and cut out three bells from white plastic-foam trays. Paint the bells with gold and silver paint. Sprinkle them with gold and silver glitter while the paint is wet and let dry.
3. Make a bow, following the directions on page 25, and glue it to the top of the wreath. With a hole punch, make a hole at the top of each bell and glue on a piece of ribbon.
4. Glue the bells to the wreath. Add yarn to the back of the wreath for a hanger.

Fabric Wall Hanging

fabric ● embroidery hoop ● rickrack ● cardboard
● cotton batting

1. Place a piece of fabric in an embroidery hoop. Trim around the edge. Glue rickrack around the rim of the hoop and let dry.
2. Cut pieces of cardboard to form a house shape that will fit inside the hoop area.
3. Glue one layer of cotton batting on top of the cardboard pieces. Cut fabric a little larger than the cardboard pieces, and wrap it around the cardboard. Glue the extra fabric to the back.
4. Glue the house to the fabric in the hoop. Decorate with pieces of fabric to make windows and a door. Add rickrack to the roof.

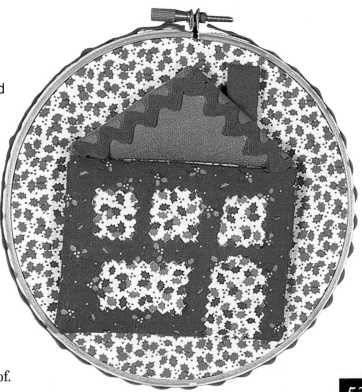

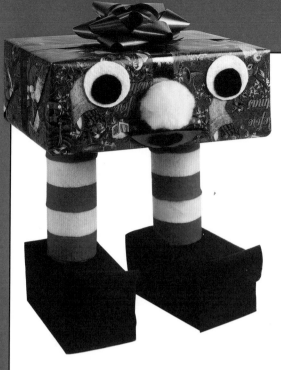

Elfin Creature

pasta box ● gift wrap ● ribbon ● stick-on bow ● felt ● large pompom ● two butter boxes ● two cardboard tubes

1. Cover a pasta box with gift wrap, ribbon, and a stick-on bow.
2. Add a face using felt for the eyes and mouth and a large pompom for a nose.
3. Cover two butter boxes with felt, making pointed toes like elf shoes.
4. Cut holes in the butter boxes and underneath the present so cardboard tubes can fit through.
5. Glue the tubes in place, and decorate with felt strips.

Paper-Plate Angel

paper plate ● chenille stick ● aluminum foil ● ribbon ● dental floss

1. To make the angel's shape, cut a paper plate as shown. Fold the plate back to make the angel's body. Fold the plate forward to make the angel's wings.
2. To make the angel's hair, wrap a chenille stick around a pencil. Slide the curled stick off the pencil, and glue it around the angel's face. Add features with markers.
3. For the gown, glue on aluminum foil. Add a ribbon bow.
4. Tie a piece of dental floss through the hair for a hanger.

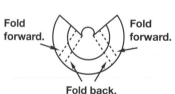

Fold forward.   Fold forward.

Fold back.

Tubular Reindeer

cardboard tube ● construction paper ● yarn ● small twigs

1. Cut four sections from one end of a cardboard tube to form the reindeer's four legs.
2. Cut eyes, a nose, and hoofs from construction paper, and glue them in place. Tie a yarn bow around the deer's neck.
3. Using a hole punch, punch a hole on each side of the reindeer's head. Push small twigs through the holes for antlers.

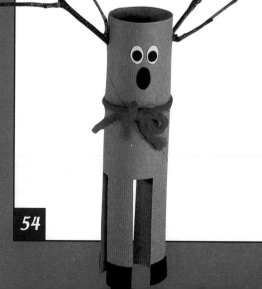

Stained-Glass Decoration

white shelf paper ● paper towels ● cotton balls ● baby oil
● poster board

1. Cut a piece of white shelf paper to fit in a window. Sketch a drawing on the panel in pencil. With black crayon, draw heavily over the lines about ¼ inch in width, creating the "leading."
2. Color each area within the leading, pressing hard on the crayon to get as deep a color and as opaque a covering as possible.
3. Turn the panel facedown on a paper-towel-covered surface. Dip a cotton ball in baby oil and rub the back of the paper. The oil gives the translucent effect of stained glass.
4. Wipe off any excess oil and let dry. Cut strips of poster board and glue them together to form a frame. Tape the stained-glass picture in the frame.

Craft-Stick Christmas Tree

craft sticks ● construction paper
● wiggle eyes ● pompoms or beads
● thread

1. Paint two craft sticks black and seven craft sticks green on both sides.
2. To make the trunk, glue the black sticks end to end.
3. To add branches, glue the green sticks along the trunk.
4. Draw a star and some birds on construction paper, and cut them out. Glue wiggle eyes on the birds.
5. Glue the star and the birds on the branches. Add pompoms or beads as ornaments.
6. After the glue dries, make a hanger by tying the ends of a piece of thread to the top branch.

Picture-Perfect Gift Tags

construction paper ● photographs ● glitter glue ● cording

1. Draw and cut holiday shapes from construction paper. With an adult's permission, cut faces of friends and family from extra photographs. Glue one face to each holiday cutout.
2. Use paper scraps to add arms, legs, hands, feet, hats, or clothing to your cutouts. Decorate with glitter glue and markers.
3. Punch a hole at the top of each card. Thread and knot cording through each hole.
4. Place the tags on the gifts you have wrapped for the people in the photos. Family and friends will know which gift is theirs by looking at the face on the tag.

Silvery Jingle Bells

cardboard egg cartons ● glitter ● string ● jingle bells

1. To make the bell shapes, cut three pillars from a cardboard egg carton. Paint them inside and out. Sprinkle them with glitter and let dry.
2. Attach a string to a jingle bell and tie a knot about an inch above it.
3. Poke a small hole in the cardboard bell and pull the string through the hole until the knot is against the inside of the cardboard bell. Tie a knot in the string on top of the cardboard bell.
4. Follow steps 2 and 3 for the other two bells. Gather all the strings together and tie a knot. Hang the bells in a window or on a door.

Festive Banner

felt ● wooden dowel ● cording

1. Place four pieces of felt vertically on your work space. Overlap the edges about 1 inch and glue them together. Fold the top edge of the first panel over a thin wooden dowel and glue in place. Let dry.
2. Cut Christmas symbols such as a candle, a bell, a tree, and a dove from pieces of felt and glue onto the panels.
3. Glue or staple cording around the ends of the dowel for a hanger.

Bead-and-Yarn Wreath

beads ● yarn

1. Thread some beads on a length of yarn.
2. Loosely wrap the yarn around your hand about twenty times to form a circle.
3. Cut eight pieces of yarn, each about 6 inches long. Tie each piece, evenly spaced, around the wreath to hold it together. Knot the ends, and trim them with scissors.
4. Decorate the wreath with a red yarn bow. For a hanger, make a loop from a piece of yarn.

Holiday Greetings Address Book

cardboard ● index cards ● fabric ● ribbon

1. To make the front and the back of the book, cut two pieces of cardboard 6½ inches by 4½ inches. Using a hole punch, punch a hole 1½ inches in from the long sides and ½ inch in from the narrow sides.
2. To make the inside pages, place a 4-inch-by-6-inch index card over the cardboard and mark the holes on the card. Place this card on top of several other cards, and punch out the holes. Create more inside pages, making sure all holes line up.
3. Cut holiday fabric to cover one side of the front and back cardboard pieces. Tape the edges on the other side. Feel the holes in the cardboard underneath the fabric, and punch them out. Trim with scissors. Glue a punched card over the taped fabric, lining up the holes.
4. Place the index cards inside the covers. Thread a piece of ribbon through the holes in the back cover, the cards, and the front cover. Tie the ribbon into a bow.

Gift Tree

large plastic-foam ball ● medium-sized clay pot ● mint containers ● yarn ● thin fallen tree branch ● paper

1. Press a large plastic-foam ball firmly into a medium-sized clay pot. Turn the pot upside down and paint it. Let dry.
2. Paint a few mint containers. Let dry. Tie yarn around the containers.
3. Paint a thin fallen tree branch white. Let dry. Stick the branch in the hole in the bottom of the pot through the foam ball.
4. Hang the "gifts" on the tree. If you like, make small tags from paper with your family's names on them and stick them on each container.

Christmas Yarn Card

construction paper ● yarn

1. Fold a piece of construction paper in half to make a card.
2. On the front of the card, draw the outline of the design you want.
3. Squeeze glue on the shape. Press bits of yarn into the glue and let it dry.
4. Write a holiday greeting inside.

Hand-and-Foot Reindeer

construction paper ● yarn

1. Trace around each of your hands onto a piece of construction paper. Cut out the shapes.
2. Trace around the bottom of one of your shoes onto another piece of construction paper. Cut out the shape.
3. Glue the base of each paper hand to one end of the paper shoe to make antlers.
4. Cut out paper eyes and a nose, and glue them in place.
5. Write a greeting on the back and give the reindeer face to someone special. Or tape a loop of yarn to the back as a hanger.

Festive Stencil Paper

newspaper ● poster paper ● poster board ● cellulose sponge ● watercolor paint

1. Cover your work surface with newspaper. Cut a large piece of poster paper and tape the corners down so the paper is flat on the newspaper.
2. To make stencils, draw and cut out holiday designs from 6-inch-square pieces of poster board as shown. Hold a stencil on the poster paper. Dip a small piece of cellulose sponge in watercolor paint and dab the inside of the stencil.
3. Let the designs dry. Use the paper to wrap holiday gifts.

Advent Candles

corrugated cardboard ● paper ● felt ● rickrack ● five cardboard tubes ● pompoms

1. To make the base, cut an 8-inch circle from corrugated cardboard. Lay the base on a piece of paper, trace around it, and cut it out. Do the same with a piece of white felt. Glue the paper and then the felt on top of the base. Glue rickrack around the edge.
2. To make the candles, glue blue felt around three cardboard tubes. Glue pink felt on one tube and white felt on another. Glue the tubes to the base.
3. Decorate around the candle bases with holly leaves cut from green felt. Add red pompoms for berries. Cut pieces of yellow felt for the candle flames. Roll pieces of tape to attach a flame to each candle.
4. Attach a flame to one blue candle on the first, second, and fourth Sundays before Christmas. Light the pink one on the third Sunday. Light the white candle on Christmas Day.

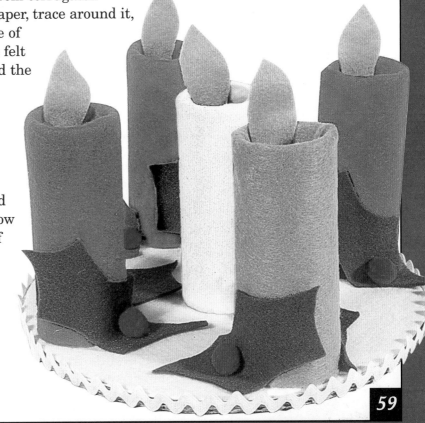

Craft-Stick Reindeer

three craft sticks ● pompom ● felt ● wiggle eyes
● construction paper ● yarn

1. Glue three craft sticks together in an A shape and let dry.
2. Turn the A shape upside down. Decorate with a pompom nose. Glue felt circles underneath wiggle eyes. Add construction paper and pompom holly leaves and berries.
3. Glue a loop of yarn to the back, and hang the reindeer on your holiday tree.

Holiday Bookmark

plain ribbon ● plaid ribbon ● old holiday greeting card

1. Glue a narrow piece of plain ribbon on top of a wide piece of plaid ribbon about 10 inches long. Cut a V shape from each end.
2. Cut a scene from an old holiday greeting card and glue it on top of the ribbons. Let dry.

Juice-Can Santa

large juice can ● felt ● cardboard ● pompom ● yarn

1. Cover the top third of a large juice can with skin-colored felt and the rest with red felt. Add a belt and a narrow strip of felt to separate the pant legs.
2. Cut a circle with feet from cardboard, cover with black felt, and glue to the bottom of the can.
3. Cut out a beard, eyes, eyebrows, and hair from felt. Snip a small hole in the beard where the mouth should be. Glue black felt over the hole, then glue everything in place. Add a pompom for a nose.
4. Cut out arms with mittens from felt and glue in place.
5. Cut out a 15½-inch-by-6-inch piece of red felt. Glue the short sides together, add white trim along one edge, and glue the hat to Santa's head. Snip around the top of the hat every ¼ inch or so to make fringe. Gather the top closed, and tie with white yarn.

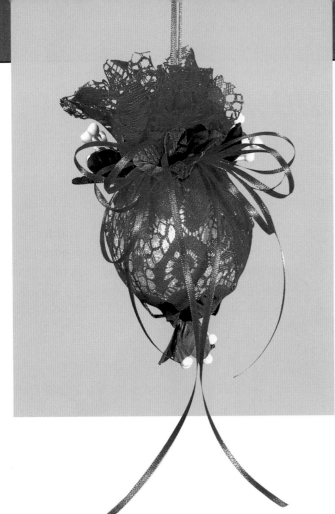

Mistletoe

3-inch plastic-foam ball ● lace ● ribbon ● plastic mistletoe ● straight pin

1. Place a 3-inch plastic-foam ball in the center of a 14-inch circle of lace.
2. Gather the lace around the ball and tie a piece of ribbon tightly to hold the lace together. Make loops from a second piece of ribbon and attach them to the first ribbon, making a knot. Leave the ribbon ends loose.
3. Poke pieces of plastic mistletoe in between the holes of the lace. Add glue to hold the leaves in position if necessary.
4. To make a hanger, cut a long piece of ribbon. Place a straight pin through the ends. Push the pin into the top of the ball.

Sock Snowman

old white tube sock ● beans ● cotton ● yarn ● construction paper ● chenille sticks ● wiggle eyes ● buttons ● felt

1. Fill the bottom of an old white tube sock 1 inch deep with beans. Fill the rest of the sock with cotton. Tie yarn around the sock in two places to form the snowman's body. Tie off the top and trim.
2. Make a hat with a strip and circles of construction paper and glue it onto the head.
3. Make a nose and a mouth from chenille sticks and glue in place. Glue on wiggle eyes. Glue buttons down the front of the snowman. Let dry.
4. Poke brown chenille sticks through the upper part of the body to make arms. Cut several pieces from another brown chenille stick and twist onto each end, forming the hands.
5. Cut a scarf from felt and glue it around the snowman's neck. Let dry.

61

Orange-Spice Potpourri

plastic container and lid ● twigs ● pinecones ● ribbon
● waxed paper ● glitter ● twine ● orange peel
● pine needles ● cinnamon sticks ● whole cloves ● paper

1. Remove the label from a clean plastic container with a lid. Use paint to color the lid.
2. Find some twigs, small pinecones, and a length of ribbon. Set them on waxed paper. Add glue and glitter. Let dry.
3. Use twine to tie the twigs in a bundle. Glue the twigs and pinecones on the lid. Glue the ribbon around the container.
4. To make potpourri, let some orange-peel pieces and pine needles air-dry for a few days, then mix them with cinnamon sticks and whole cloves. Fill the container with potpourri and put on the lid.
5. Make a gift tag from paper and twine. Use markers to decorate it. Write "Orange-Spice Potpourri" on the front and "Simmer a handful in water over low heat" on the back. Add a personal message.

Santa Bell

pencil ● red electrical tape ● jingle bell ● twist tie
● red paper ● cotton ● glitter glue

1. Wrap a pencil with red electrical tape.
2. Slide a jingle bell onto the center of a twist tie. Twist the twist tie together to hold the bell in place. Leave a bit of the twist-tie ends untwisted. Place the ends on either side of the pencil point and tape them to the pencil.
3. Draw and cut a half circle from red paper. Fold the half circle into a cone shape around the bell end of the pencil and secure with tape.
4. Glue cotton around the top of the cone for Santa's hat. Draw eyes below the cotton with marker. Place a red glitter-glue nose below the eyes. Stretch a piece of cotton into a beard and glue the beard below the nose. Roll a tiny piece of cotton into a mustache and glue it at the top of the beard. Glue cotton around the bottom of the cone. Glue a small ball of cotton to the top of the pencil.

Holiday Stamp Card

used postage stamps ● pan ● water ● newspaper
● construction paper ● white paper

1. Cut used postage stamps from envelopes and place them in a pan of water until the stamp separates from the paper. Lay the stamps facedown on newspaper to dry.
2. Draw and cut out a construction-paper tree.
3. Cut the stamps in half diagonally. Glue them inside the lines of the tree.
4. Glue the tree to a folded piece of construction paper to make a card. Decorate the card.
5. Glue a piece of white paper inside the card and write a holiday greeting.

Filter Flakes

waxed paper ● coffee filters ● cups ● water ● food coloring
● spoon ● thread

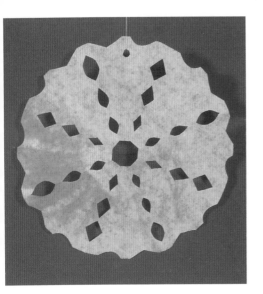

1. Place some waxed paper on a waterproof work surface. On the waxed paper make three stacks of three coffee filters each.
2. Fill three cups with water. Add a few drops of food coloring to each cup.
3. With a spoon, add drops of colored water to each stack of filters. Let the filters dry, then separate the stacks.
4. To make a snowflake, fold a filter in half. Fold it in half again, then fold it in half once more.
5. Cut off the pointed top from the folded filter. Then cut out small, unconnected triangles and half circles from along the edges of the folded filter.
6. Unfold the filter. Punch a hole at the edge of the snowflake, and hang it with thread.

Reindeer Pin

small plastic toy container ● brown yarn ● brown chenille sticks
● wiggle eyes ● red pompom ● safety pin

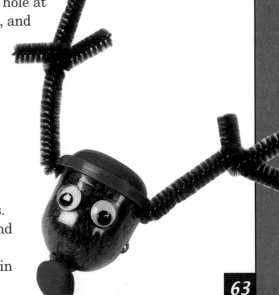

1. Fill a small plastic toy container with brown yarn.
2. Cut two small pieces from a brown chenille stick. Twist the pieces onto each end of another chenille stick to create antlers. Place the center of the antlers over the top of the container, and snap the lid over the antlers, securing them in place.
3. Glue on wiggle eyes and a pompom for a nose. Glue a safety pin to the back of the reindeer. Let dry.

Index